This Journal Belongs to:

ELEVATE

A Journal to Push Beyond Your

Limits and Unlock Success

in Yourself and Others

ROBERT GLAZER

simple truths
▶ Small books. BIG IMPACT.

Published by Simple Truths, an imprint of Sourcebooks
P.O. Box 4410, Naperville, Illinois 60567-4410
(630) 961-3900
sourcebooks.com

Printed and bound in the United States of America.
POD 10 9 8 7 6 5 4 3 2 1

For everyone who knows deep
down they can be more.

For Chloe, Max, and Zach.
You each inspire me to be better every day.

INTRODUCTION

Have you ever wondered why some individuals are consistently able to achieve at such a high level?

They are always pushing forward and hitting their goals. They seem to be doing more with less, while the rest of us spin our wheels but don't make as much progress. The same is true with organizations. It might be comforting to believe they have some advantage over you, when the truth is they have found a way to become an elevated version of themselves.

In 2015, I started sending an inspirational email every Friday to the people at my company, Acceleration Partners, which I later named "Friday Forward" (www.fridayfwd.com). Rather than focus the content on business-related topics, I hoped to provide inspiration around the concept of personal improvement and growth. My goal was to encourage our employees to want to achieve more in all areas of their life. I wanted to help them challenge their self-limiting beliefs and realize their true potential, something that very much aligned to my core values.

I thought my Friday emails would be skimmed, at best, and maybe even ignored. To my surprise, employees told me they looked forward to the messages each week and shared them with friends and family. The weekly emails also had a noticeable impact within our company, as people started taking action and applying the different concepts in their work and lives. In just a few short years, these weekly messages had spread to over one hundred thousand people across fifty countries and were shared across and within companies.

In creating and sharing the Friday Forward emails, my initial goal was to inspire and motivate others. However, I soon came to realize a deeper truth.

By tackling these concepts and having the discipline to write about them each week, I was pushing myself to perform better and grow my *own* capacity, my ability to achieve and perform consistently at a higher level. Inspiration of others was the catalyst, and my journey of personal growth and achievement was the effect.

I could see my Friday Forward messages were helping others in life and at work. Our team members began reaching new personal and professional heights simultaneously. They were running races, getting healthier, committing more quality time to family, traveling abroad and outside their comfort zones, and creating positive examples for one another. By taking a holistic approach to inspiring our team, we saw a higher return on investment than we did by just helping them get better at their current jobs.

The same was true of people who would write back to me each week from across the world and share their stories and experiences of growth and achievement.

I could tell I was making a difference, but I wasn't as clear about how. So I dug into the themes of my writing and quickly realized the patterns that illuminated the four elements of capacity building. Soon, I had a simple framework for changing my life, growing my business, and improving both the lives of employees and strangers.

Be forewarned, *Elevate*, the companion book to this journal, isn't a scientific book with academic studies and theories. It's a book full of real-world results, time-tested principles, and actionable advice designed in a format that you can keep on your desk or bedside table and dive into at different points based on where you are on your capacity-building journey at any point in time.

I am excited to share this framework, which has served as a personal road map to higher achievement. I believe it is the key to elevating and achieving things both in life and business that you never thought possible.

WHAT IS
CAPACITY BUILDING?

In its purest definition, capacity building is the method by which individuals seek, acquire, and develop the skills and abilities to consistently perform at a higher level in pursuit of their innate potential.

High achievers across all spectrums of life and business have found continuous ways to build their capacity at faster rates than their peers and use that extra capacity to stay ahead of the pack and achieve at a high level; it's how they elevate. People who consistently elevate, or "elevaters," have a competitive advantage. But it's one that you can replicate.

To be clear, capacity building is not about doing more. It's about doing more of the right things. In fact, the art of the capacity-building process is knowing where you need to invest your energy and where you need to pull away.

As the legendary management guru Peter Drucker

once wrote, "There is surely nothing quite so useless as doing with great efficiency what should not be done at all."

Capacity building is similar to developing a muscle. It doesn't happen overnight. I may be inspired to lift a heavy weight, but only after weeks of consistent commitment, work, and incremental improvement will I have built up the strength and physical capacity to do so. Suddenly, I have the capacity to do what I could not do before. Inspiration is valuable, but it's not enough to affect real change. That requires follow-though and commitment.

In my own journey and in speaking with hundreds of others who have made meaningful and sustained changes to their lives, I have identified four essential elements of capacity building: spiritual, intellectual, physical, and emotional. These four elements are fundamental and are present in nearly every aspect of self-improvement.

1. **Spiritual capacity** is about understanding who you are, what you want most, and the standards you want to live by each day.

2. **Intellectual capacity** is about how you improve your ability to think, learn, plan, and execute with discipline.

3. **Physical capacity** is your health, well-being, and physical performance.

4. **Emotional capacity** is how you react to challenging situations, your emotional mindset, and the quality of your relationships.

Capacity building starts with understanding these four interconnected elements and then developing them individually and simultaneously. A leader's goal should be to inspire and elevate expectations so that team members can simultaneously improve in all areas of their lives, including leadership, time management, prioritization, decision-making, self-awareness, and self-confidence. These abilities have a domino effect. When you improve in one area, you begin to improve in all. And one of the most important outcomes in capacity building is the exponential effect it has on others, including friends, family, and those whom you lead. It has the effect of lifting while you climb—as you build your own capacity and achieve more, you develop the ability to help others do the same.

It's a virtuous cycle and benefits everyone involved.

By focusing on these elements, you'll be on a path to build your own capacity to elevate and support others in their journey as well.

BUILD YOUR
SPIRITUAL CAPACITY

The term *spiritual* is often used in the context of religion or things that are intangible, but in the context of capacity building, it means something different.

At its core, spiritual capacity is about understanding who you are and what you want most for your life. It's the process of developing your North Star and the principles that guide your actions and shape your major decisions. Building your spiritual capacity is really a journey of self-actualization, a path of discovery about the unique motivations that you have within you. It's the motor that is driving you, either unconsciously or consciously.

Great companies have clear visions of where they want to go, an enduring purpose, as well as clearly established core values. These same principles apply to living a great life.

With a company, the vision is usually easier to decipher.

It's often the reason the company was started in the first place (e.g., the founder wanted to disrupt transportation or eradicate cancer). The core values are often developed over time, as they represent the collective values of team members.

With individuals, the inverse is true; it's easier for us to first identify our core values. It's very unlikely you entered this world as a baby understanding and able to clearly articulate the purpose or vision for your life. This is a concept many of us don't begin to contemplate until our thirties or forties, but the sooner you start, the better.

The only way you can build your spiritual capacity is to take time to deeply reflect on what matters most to you. Ask yourself some of these questions: What would you work unpaid for? What are you doing when you feel fully engaged? When are you not at your best? What sort of values or characteristics do others have that drive you crazy? Write them down and start to draw lines between similar concepts.

Start Your Core Values List

Your core values are the guideposts that influence your behavior and decision-making, even when you don't realize it. Revisit the time you spent reflecting last week and make a list of words or phrases that fit with your answers—things like compassionate, fair, independent, consistent. Write down as many as you see fit—you will condense the list later.

One of the best ways we can build our spiritual capacity is to seek insight from people who know us best. Whether it's a family member, spouse, partner, or close friend, ask them the same questions that you asked yourself about when you are at your best and when you struggle or are unhappy. Get their feedback and then share your notes. Take note of their responses and see if their input makes you reevaluate your list.

A great way to evaluate your progress in building your spiritual capacity is to learn from experts on the topic. Two examples that I've found especially enlightening are *True North* by Bill George and *Man's Search for Meaning* by Viktor Frankl—these will challenge you to rethink your work so far and help you serve your purpose and values each day. Also, listen to Warren Rustand's episode on the *Elevate* podcast to get inspiration on building a purpose-driven life: www.robertglazer.com/warren

Having taken the time to write down a long list of potential core values, here's the more challenging part—take careful thought of each one and determine whether it belongs on your top five most important core values list. A good way to start is by seeing which words could be combined into one concept. For example, you may have both fairness and equality on your list—combine those two into one to help shorten your list. If you aren't sure whether something belongs on the list, ask yourself, "Would I make a big life decision based on this value?"

This is a common, but effective, self-actualization activity. Write a few paragraphs about how you'd like to be remembered in an obituary. What do you want to achieve? How do you want to impact others? This is a good way to evaluate if your core values are a good fit; what you want to be remembered for is likely what's most important to you.

Begin to Think about Your Core Purpose

Your core purpose is like the topic sentence for your life—it's difficult to articulate it, but once you know your purpose, you won't spend time running in the wrong direction. There are multiple resources that can help you contemplate your core purpose, such as Simon Sinek's website and materials or Why Institute. You can also consider if your purpose stems from a place of pain or an early childhood experience. Here's a great Friday Forward on the topic: https://www.robertglazer.com/friday-forward/purpose-and-pain/.

Draft a Purpose Statement

You don't have to be 100 percent certain of your purpose at this point—building spiritual capacity is a long journey, and you need to give yourself the space to adjust and make changes. But for now, challenge yourself to think of a purpose statement for life, and think carefully about if it feels right for you. Remember, what matters most is if that purpose fulfills *you*.

One of the best things about finding our purpose and core values is that it gives us clarity on what things in life aren't helping us get toward our final destination. Take stock of things you do—either professional or personally—and make a list of five things that you will commit to stop doing over the next three to six months. Put the wheels in motion on one or more of them this week. For more inspiration and examples on this concept, check out robertglazer.com/stop.

Part of building your spiritual capacity is making sure you're working toward your purpose and values in your daily life. I have a tool I love to use called the Whole Life Dashboard—try downloading the template, filling in your core values, and brainstorming how you can set goals that build toward them. Get started at robertglazer.com/wld/.

Read These Three Friday Forwards of Values

Friday Forward is a great resource for inspiration and helpful anecdotes on capacity building. To help hone your spiritual capacity, try reading these three, and write down your reaction to each.

Raising Values: robertglazer.com/friday-forward/raising-values/

An Incredible Eulogy: robertglazer.com/friday-forward/an-incredible-eulogy/

Moment of Clarity: robertglazer.com/friday-forward/moment-of-clarity/

Commit to Your Purpose and Values

Write down your core purpose and top five core values on a sheet of paper, then add a description of each underneath. Put it on your desk so you can see it every day.

A huge benefit of capacity building is the impact you can have on others. If you've been able to find some answers by building your spiritual capacity, try reaching out to somebody close to you and see if they'd like your help doing the same.

BUILD YOUR INTELLECTUAL CAPACITY

Intellectual capacity is about how you improve your ability to think, learn, plan, and execute with discipline. It is closely correlated with the area of your brain called the *frontal lobe*, which acts as the control panel for many of your executive functions.

Think of intellectual capacity as your personal processor/operating system that can be continuously upgraded to perform the same tasks smarter, faster, or more efficiently than before. The greater your intellectual capacity, the greater your level of achievement with the same or less expenditure of energy.

This element of capacity building can offer the greatest opportunity for immediate gains, but it also requires the most discipline.

Embrace a Growth Mindset

A key to building your intellectual capacity is believing that you are capable of doing it. You need to challenge yourself to think of your limitations as temporary. Start by making a list of your self-limiting beliefs, then rephrase them as opportunities to grow. For example, change "I hate being corrected" to "Feedback helps me improve." Adjust "This is too difficult" to say "If I work hard, I can achieve this." Revisit this list whenever you feel doubts.

Generally speaking, you'll rarely be given exactly the knowledge you need at the right time—you need to be proactive and seek it out. Pick a topic you'd like to learn more about—something broad, like marketing, psychology, or nutrition—and research the top authors and books on that topic. Order one or two of them. Also research podcasts on the same topic and download them to your phone. Finally, check out popular book summary sites such as blinkist.com, soundview.com, and getabstract.com, as well as the Blinkist App, which summarizes the top themes of many books on audio.

It's easier to learn when you're working with others—even connecting with just one other person is a great way to hold yourself accountable to your commitments, share your ideas with another person, and get somebody else's perspective. This will broaden your viewpoint and focus your thinking. Plan to touch base even for just fifteen minutes at the end of each week and review what you each committed to for the week. That simple call will keep you on task. You can also do this via email if you add it as a commitment in your calendar.

You've already identified books that can help you learn something new, but sometimes it takes an extra push to actually get started—consider this that push. Buy or borrow a book you want to read and get started—if you want to challenge yourself, try setting aside thirty to sixty minutes each day this week to reading it. Either first thing in the morning or right before bed are two great options.

THIS WEEK...
Start a Journal

Journaling is a great activity that allows you to hold your-self accountable for what you are doing each day to pursue your goals. *The Five Minute Journal* is a great example of a daily journal that will help you hold yourself accountable each day.

People with high intellectual capacity don't just let things happen to them—they take control of their lives and recognize when they need to make a proactive change. Take some time to evaluate where you've plateaued—either personally or professionally—and brainstorm proactive changes you can make. Resolve to learn a new skill, find and join a class about something new, or register for a conference in your field—do something proactive that will help you grow. And once you find it, pay for it now.

A common mistake is to set several goals that either don't relate to each other or don't serve your purpose and core values. You cannot derive purpose from your goals—you have to set goals that pursue the purpose you've found. If you already have a list of goals for the next year, five years, or ten years, now is the time to evaluate whether they are actually what you want and if they are aligned. Start backwards from ten years and think about your short-term goals in terms of small down payments on what it will take to get there.

Working with a peer is often helpful, but sometimes you need expertise from a person who has experienced more than you have. Give some thought to people in your life—a high-achieving friend, an esteemed colleague, or another connection—who could serve as a mentor to you, and ask them to grab a coffee or a drink. I personally have relied on many mentors and coaches over the years, and the more time and effort you dedicate to cultivating those relationships, the more you'll grow.

Get Up Fifteen Minutes Earlier and Start a Morning Routine

You can't win the day within an hour of waking up, but you can lose it. High-achievers tend to wake up early, because it gives them time to do a set routine and find their focus and intention for the day—before the rest of the world is awake and distracting them. Challenge yourself to wake up even fifteen minutes earlier than usual each day this week. And don't look at your email or smartphone; instead, spend that time meditating, reading, or journaling. Write down how you feel throughout the day as a result.

Take a look at the goals you created a few weeks back and make sure they are SMART: Specific, Measurable, Attainable, Realistic, and Timely. A good way to think of this is to set a goal that measures your input rather than an outcome. For example, rather than saying, "I want to lose twenty pounds," instead say, "I want to exercise four times per week." This way, you are changing your habit rather than pursuing an arbitrary number without a clear strategy to get there.

Habits are a key to building discipline in your daily life. Pick something productive that you resolve to do each day this week, even if it's something simple like starting the day with a full glass of water or doing fifty push-ups before your morning shower. If you instill these kinds of habits into your daily life, you'll find you have more energy and focus during the day, even if it's just a little bit at first. Resolve to carry that habit into next week as well, and build your momentum. A great way to make a new habit stick is to stack it. For example, if you have coffee every morning, do those fifty push-ups while it is brewing.

To grow, it's crucial to be proactive and commit to the execution of a plan. People who have big ideas and goals, but who don't actually do anything about them, don't have high intellectual capacity. So put some money on the line: sign up for something that requires even a small deposit, like a race you want to run, a class you want to take, or even a vacation you've wanted for years. You need to familiarize yourself with the positive feeling of committing to something and actually doing it—once you do it, you'll want to chase that feeling in other facets of life.

Just like with spiritual capacity, you can use your own growth to help others, and there is someone out there that could use your guidance. Look for mentoring opportunities within your network, through nonprofits, or at your job. You can make an impact well beyond yourself and learn a lot in the process.

BUILD YOUR PHYSICAL CAPACITY

Physical capacity is your ability to improve your health, well-being, and physical performance. While your brain helps drive and guide you through life, it's your body that is asked to do most of the heavy lifting, day in and day out.

While we understand the concept of building physical strength and endurance, we often overlook the other aspects of being healthy, particularly the connection between our brains and our bodies. Fortunately, this correlation is gaining far more awareness.

Your physical capacity acts as either an accelerant or a drag on your overall quest to build capacity. When your physical capacity is strong, you have more endurance and resilience. You rise to the occasion. You also learn and process faster (intellectual capacity) and feel better about yourself and have more to give to others (emotional capacity). When your physical capacity is not strong, doing almost anything is harder, if not impossible.

Symptoms such as fatigue and stress significantly affect your immunity and how you feel day to day. The same is true of your food choices, which serve as the fuel for both your mind and body. Often, these factors work against the other positive things you are doing to increase your physical capacity.

Your health and physical capacity are more holistic concepts than you realize.

Too many people consider sleep to be an unnecessary luxury, or even a sign of weakness. In reality, it's vital to your ability to perform well, cope with stress, and be healthy overall. The distractions that keep you from sleeping will always be there, so you need to be proactive about blocking off time to unwind at the end of the day. That means shutting off your technology an hour before your scheduled bedtime and committing to getting eight hours of sleep each night.

You don't have to overhaul your entire diet to start living healthier. A good step is being aware of what you actually eat—so many of us have so much on our figurative plate, we can lose track of what's on our literal one. As a start, try writing down everything you eat this week, and even make a note of whether that meal is something you commonly eat or if it's a more rare indulgence. Also note how you felt that day or the next. You will be able to revisit this to understand your eating habits later, and you may find some patterns that suggest needed changes

Once you've made a list of what a typical week looks like, it's time to test your willpower. Try removing something unhealthy from your diet for a week and see how it makes you feel. Whether you're cutting sugar out for a week or limiting your alcohol intake, even a small change can make a difference in a short amount of time. Make sure to write down how the change makes you feel, and log the results of your alteration.

Regardless of what your starting point is, building some cardiovascular activity into your routine is a good way to improve your health and raise your energy. Every bit counts—if you don't want to start with something high-impact like jogging, try taking a brisk walk for thirty or sixty minutes each day or attend a spin class. If doing that seems like a waste of time, trying listening to the *Elevate* podcast so you can learn while you work out. And if you want to challenge yourself further, look into a high-intensity interval training, or HIIT, workout. These are shorter but have huge health benefits.

Realistically, the difficult part of launching an exercise routine isn't the start—it's keeping up the momentum and accountability. As with all aspects of capacity building, it's helpful to lean on others to help you grow. Start by picking a person close to your fitness level and making a commitment with them to hold each other accountable, exercise together occasionally, and update each other on your progress. Don't try to compare yourself to their outcomes, like who can lose more weight or run a faster mile time. Instead, compare your inputs, making sure you're matching their time and commitment to building physical capacity.

This is an easy one: just keep a log of how much water you drink each day. Hydration is vital to health regardless of your lifestyle, so whether you count the number of glasses your drink or get more scientific and measure it in ounces or gallons, keep a log. Many sources recommend drinking eight 8-ounce glasses of water a day, so see if you're meeting that standard. For an extra challenge, try cutting out a beverage like soda or juice and replacing it with water. It will also keep you fuller.

Stress is reaching epidemic levels, especially for high-performers who have many demands on their time. Just like with sleep, you need to proactively schedule time during the day to step away from work and build in some recovery time. This week, put it in your calendar. Whether you block off fifteen minutes for silent meditation several times a day or schedule a couple thirty-minute blocks to go outside and take a walk, you need to ensure you have a chance to unplug and recover. Notice if you have more energy and focus after your breaks.

This doesn't mean to only focus on yourself and ignore the responsibilities you have to other people. But in order to be your best for other people, you need to take control of your schedule and your environment. You can and should give your time to others, but I find it helpful to schedule that time, set clear boundaries for what you can and can't do, and be clear about those parameters. Say "no thanks" to something you really don't want to do. Try blocking off time in your schedule for uninterrupted work time, breaks, and time with friends and family—and see how that sense of structure makes you feel.

A significant part of achieving anything worthwhile is overcoming adversity and obstacles along the way. You need to discover what you're capable of in the face of adversity and channel that into your daily life. For inspiration on this, listen to the *Elevate* podcast with Alex Hutchinson at robertglazer.com/hutchinson/.

THIS WEEK...
Invest in Health and Wellness

As covered under the intellectual capacity section, it's helpful to give yourself an incentive to get involved in a wellness activity. Whether you join a gym, purchase classes from a yoga studio, or register to run a race, do something that will make you commit to investing in your health and wellness. It's also great to find something with a built-in deadline. Find a local 5K, half marathon, or endurance race, and pay the entry fee. It will keep you motivated to practice.

Listen to Sean Swarner on the *Elevate* Podcast

I was lucky to sit down with Sean Swarner, an inspiring endurance sportsman who will make you rethink your own physical limits. Sean survived cancer twice as a teenager, and despite only having one functional lung, he has climbed the highest mountain on each continent and reached the North and South Poles. Listen to Sean's story, and think about what limits you can push in yourself: robertglazer .com/Swarner.

While digging into intellectual capacity, we talked about the value of building SMART goals—apply that knowledge to set some measurable health goals for yourself. Remember, don't focus as hard on outcomes. Instead, challenge yourself to think of what changes you'll make in your actions. Whether you're committing to exercise four times per week, challenging yourself to try a new wellness activity like yoga, or pledging to run a marathon next year, log that goal and pursue it.

When you get on course to build physical capacity, you can inspire others to do the same. Reach out to somebody who you know is interested in taking some positive steps on their physical capacity and offer to help. Whether you're sharing what's worked for you, or just offering to be an accountability partner, a little goes a long way.

BUILD YOUR EMOTIONAL CAPACITY

Your level of emotional capacity is deeply connected with how you manage the little voice in your head, interact with others, and the quality of your relationships.

When you see two people of seemingly equal intellectual and physical capacity achieving very different outcomes, it is quite likely due to an imbalance in emotional capacity.

None of us exist in a vacuum. We live in a world in which our actions, interactions, and experiences are interwoven into the lives and actions of others. The quality of our relationships and the energy gained or consumed by these relationships is extremely powerful.

Think about a race car. If your spiritual, physical, and intellectual capacities are the tools to design, build, and improve the car, your emotional capacity is your ability to actually drive it in the presence of other drivers and unintended obstacles.

How you react and relate to the other cars will ultimately determine if your car performs above or below its factory specifications.

For most of us, it is the missing piece in our quest to build capacity and is often the most difficult, because it extends beyond the control of our own four walls.

We are often held back by the belief that we cannot do something. What is most challenging is when we accept those limits as immovable or when we are affected by limiting beliefs without realizing it. Pick a goal you have wanted to achieve but where you have either had doubts or made excuses. Write down five reasons you think you cannot do it. Then, respond to each limit with a strategy to combat it. For example, a person who wants to write a book may say, "I don't have time to write." A good response would be to write, "I will set aside an hour each week to plan and write." Try this with whatever goal you're targeting.

A huge part of building emotional capacity is opening yourself up to discomfort. We achieve more when we expose ourselves to things beyond our comfort zone, whether that's chasing a goal that's a bit scary, entering an unfamiliar social situation, trying a new activity, or traveling somewhere new. Pick something that you don't normally do—it can be as simple as trying a totally new food for dinner or taking a new route when you walk. Or you can try something more ambitious, like making a cold call, asking someone out, or going to an event where you don't really know anyone. Reflect on how it feels to push yourself.

If you think about any person who has changed your life—be it a family member, friend, colleague, or teacher—they probably didn't impact you by just telling you what you wanted to hear all the time. To grow, you need to recognize your deficiencies and seek out advice on where you need to improve. Pick a person that you trust, either in your personal or professional life, and ask them for clear, respectful, direct feedback on something you want to do better. Then thank them for their honesty, and think about how you can improve.

THIS WEEK...
Count (and Write) Your Blessings

There's a reason why so many successful people approach every challenge believing they will overcome it. Mindset is invaluable to capacity building, and those who are grateful for what they have and see adversity as an opportunity to grow will get further than those who crumble under pressure. Take some time each day this week to write down the things you are grateful for in life—your morning routine is a great time to do this. Then, take note of how it affects your mood, energy, and ability to focus.

Our emotional capacity depends a lot on who we spend our time with. Not only does that mean putting time and effort into the relationships that fulfill you, but it also means working to build new partnerships. Make an initial list of the twenty most important relationships in your personal and professional life. The Whole Life Dashboard (robertglazer .com/wld) has a Relationship Dashboard tab where you can keep track of the most valuable people in your life, including those you want to connect with in the future. Fill that out and keep it as a barometer of how you spend your relationship time.

THIS WEEK...
Focus on Giving, Not Getting

The biggest mistake we can make in relationship building is going into every interaction wondering how we can maximize our gain from it. Instead, researchers like Adam Grant have found that it is givers who end up accomplishing the most. Make a list of people you frequently interact with, personally and professionally, and write down ideas for what you can do to help each of them, or make a valuable introduction for another person this week.

We all have people in our lives who are frustrating to be around, who often blame others for their misfortune and never try to help others. You've probably noticed that when you spend time with these people, you leave the experience feeling tired and drained. They are energy vampires. Are there people in your life who make you feel this way? If so, write down their names and think about how you can minimize your interactions with them. Don't burn the bridge or push them away, just be careful about how much of your time and attention you give them. Maybe it's as simple as pushing a call or get-together back a few weeks or not suggesting you should "catch-up" when you really don't want to.

THIS WEEK...
Be Vulnerable

By now, you've had a lot of time to think about the people you value and trust the most. When you're with them, whether one-on-one or in a group, take a chance and share something vulnerable about yourself. Be honest about a doubt or fear you have or share something you've done—or not done—that you regret. Not only will doing this help you grow from the experience, but it will likely also start a dialogue that could change your relationship for the better. You could also do the same on social media: post something outside of your life highlight reel, which is what comprises 99 percent of the messages that you read.

Start Reading *Mistakes Were Made (But Not by Me)*

One of the most powerful forces that limits our emotional capacity is cognitive dissonance. This term describes a situation where we hold two or more contradictory views or ideas in our mind at once. Understanding this force and how it can compel us to not try something new, double down on unhelpful behavior, or invest in relationships that hurt us, is important. Start with *Mistakes Were Made (But Not by Me)* by Carol Tarvis and Elliot Aronson. It will change your perspective.

This week, put a real focus on ignoring all things outside your control, whether it's the weather, the news, the stock market, global warming, or other people's behavior. If you don't control it, ignore it this week and instead focus on what you do control. See if you notice a difference in your mindset and approach.

Travel is one of the best ways to grow emotional capacity—it exposes us to new surroundings, forces us to deviate from our daily routines, and pushes us to explore and figure out a new location. If you can, travel to a foreign country, especially one with a different national language—that is particularly helpful—but even if you just pick a place that's new, that counts too.

To get inspiration on building your emotional capacity, including how you can manage your emotional reactions and stay away from negative relationships that drain your energy, read these three Friday Forwards:

robertglazer.com/friday-forward/energy-vampires/

robertglazer.com/friday-forward/bad-week/

robertglazer.com/friday-forward/controlling-reactions/

Once again, it's vital to use your capacity-building journey to help others do the same for themselves. Whether you are helping a person set goals beyond their comfort zone, challenging them to fight through their limiting beliefs, or offering valuable, candid feedback, help somebody else build their emotional capacity.

NOTES...

NOTES...

NOTES...

NOTES...

NOTES...

NOTES...

NOTES...

NOTES...

ABOUT
THE AUTHOR

Robert Glazer is the founder and CEO of global performance marketing agency Acceleration Partners. A serial entrepreneur, Bob has a passion for helping individuals and organizations build their capacity to elevate.

Under his leadership, Acceleration Partners has received numerous industry and company culture awards, including Glassdoor's Employees' Choice Awards (two years in a row), *Ad Age*'s Best Place to Work, *Entrepreneur*'s Top Company Culture (two years in a row), Great Place to Work and *Fortune*'s Best Small and Medium Workplaces (three years in a row), and *Boston Globe*'s Top Workplaces (two years in a row). Bob was also named to Glassdoor's list of Top CEOs of Small and Medium Companies in the U.S., ranking number two.

A regular columnist for *Forbes*, *Inc.*, and *Entrepreneur*, Bob's writing reaches over five million people around the globe each year who resonate with his topics, which range from performance marketing and entrepreneurship to company culture, capacity building, hiring, and leadership. Worldwide, he is also a sought-after speaker by companies and organizations on subjects related to business growth, culture, building capacity, and performance.

Bob shares his ideas and insights via Friday Forward, a popular weekly inspirational newsletter that reaches over one hundred thousand individuals and business leaders across over fifty countries. He is also the author of the international bestselling book *Performance Partnerships.*

Looking for more?

For resources on each capacity: robertglazer.com/elevate-resources/

For Friday Forwards on Spiritual Capacity: robertglazer.com/category/spiritual/

For Friday Forwards on Intellectual Capacity: robertglazer.com/category/intellectual/

For Friday Forwards on Physical Capacity: robertglazer.com/category/physical/

For Friday Forwards on Emotional Capacity: robertglazer.com/category/emotional/

To hear interviews with the world's leading CEOs, authors, and thinkers on capacity building, try the *Elevate* podcast: robertglazer.com/elevate-podcast/